# Scriptural Meditations for the Divine Mercy Chaplet Franciscan Crown Seven Sorrows and Rosary

*Lucas J. Amato, S.F.O.*

***Scriptural Meditations for the Divine Mercy Chaplet, Franciscan Crown, Seven Sorrows, and Rosary***

Devised and compiled by Lucas J. Amato, S.F.O.
Edited by Gregory F. Augustine Pierce
Cover by Tom A. Wright
Text design and typesetting by Desktop Edit Shop



Previously published by ACTA Publications, 2009.

Printed in the United States of America.

9131

978-1-64121-010-2

# *Table of Contents*

# *Introduction*

The Divine Mercy Chaplet, the Franciscan Crown of Mary's Seven Joys, and the Seven Sorrows of Mary (the Servite Chaplet) are additional devotions that can be said using the beads of the rosary. This booklet offers instructions for praying each of these devotions, as well as the traditional (Dominican) Rosary, using passages from Scripture to focus our meditations on each mystery presented.

Don't you share my problems with meditating on the mysteries of the life of Jesus and Mary? I lose my concentration so easily. Sure, I start off fairly well at the beginning of each mystery; but before I realize it I've drifted off into thinking about some upcoming chore, such as my shopping list or some needed repairs at home.

Let's look to St. Dominic and St. Francis of Assisi for guidance to improve our meditation. These two great saints were well acquainted with each other during their lifetimes upon the earth. In fact, so high was their regard for one another and their respective missions that they seriously considered forming one single religious order. Although they ultimately decided that the Lord wanted them to remain separate, both orders retain a close fraternal relationship. In fact, to this very day a Franciscan is often invited to lead the celebration of St. Dominic's feast day for the Dominicans; likewise, a Dominican usually presides over the Mass on St. Francis' feast day for the Franciscans.

What was it that drew these men and their respective orders toward each other? Certainly among other things it was their great love of Holy Scripture and a deep devotion to Our Blessed Lady. Therefore, why don't we combine our prayers with sections from the Bible that apply to those mysteries?

You will be happy to learn that I have found at least ten verses from the Bible that deal with each mystery, even appropriating the *Magnificat* from St. Luke for the Assumption of Mary and *The Book of Revelation's* "woman clothed with the sun" for her Coronation. Thus this booklet shows you how to read a quotation from Scripture before reciting each prayer of these four devotions. This method has enabled me to continually meditate on the specific mystery and still devoutly pray the intervening prayers. For me now, each prayer becomes the melody and the Bible verses the words to my spiritual song.

Come now, let us together pray with Holy Scripture the Divine Mercy Chaplet, the Franciscan Crown, the Seven Sorrows, and the Rosary.

# *The Divine Mercy Chaplet*

The Divine Mercy Chaplet, or the Chaplet of Divine Mercy, is a relatively new form of devotion, but it has theological roots tracing back to the Old and New Testaments. Recent though it may be, it has spread with amazing speed throughout the world. For this purpose God chose as His unlikely instrument a young Polish nun, then called Sister Faustina, now revered as Saint Faustina. From 1931 through 1938, she received messages from Jesus and was asked to be a model and apostle of his mercy.

The message of Divine Mercy that Faustina received was meant not only for her personal spiritual advancement but for all of us. Our Lord even requested that His image be painted for us in accord with her visions.

She was instructed to keep a diary, *Divine Mercy in My Soul,* which has become the basis for the devotion to God's Mercy. This devotion can take the form of a novena, or a prayer (said preferably at 3:00 P.M. each day), or the recitation of a chaplet of five decades, said on traditional rosary beads. The latter is the format which is presented here.

This devotion has culminated in the establishment of the Feast of Divine Mercy, which is celebrated throughout the Church on the First Sunday after Easter.

Because the Divine Mercy Chaplet has five decades of ten prayers each, the traditional rosary beads are perfect for saying this devotion. Instead of saying the Our Father, ten Hail Marys and a Glory Be on each decade, however, we say the special prayers passed on to us by Saint Faustina.

## *Praying the Divine Mercy Chaplet Using Rosary Beads and Scripture*

1. On the crucifix, make the sign of the cross while saying: "In the name of the Father, and of the Son, and of the Holy Spirit. Amen."
2. On the first bead, pray the following opening prayer: *You expired, Jesus, but the source of life gushed forth for souls, and the ocean of mercy opened up for the whole world. O Fount of Life, unfathomable Divine Mercy, envelop the whole world and empty Yourself out upon us.* Then repeat three times: *O Blood and Water, which gushed forth from the Heart of Jesus as a fount of mercy for us, I trust in You.*
3. On the next three beads, pray one Our Father, one Hail Mary, and the Apostles' Creed.
4. On the first bead of each of the five mysteries, announce the name of the mystery and pray the opening prayer.
5. Then, aloud or silently, read one verse from Scripture and pray the mercy prayer on each bead, as follows.

### The Agony in the Garden

*Eternal Father, I Offer You the Body and Blood, Soul and Divinity of Your Dearly Beloved Son, Our Lord Jesus Christ, in Atonement for Our Sins and Those of the Whole World.*

1. "And they went to a place which was called Gethsemane; and He said to his disciples: 'Sit here while I pray.'" Mark 14:32

*For the Sake of His Sorrowful Passion,*
*Have Mercy on Us and on the Whole World.*

2. "And He took with Him Peter, James and John and began to be greatly distressed and troubled. 'My soul is sor-

rowful, even unto death.'" Mark 14:33-34

*For the Sake of His Sorrowful Passion,*
*Have Mercy on Us and on the Whole World.*

3. "'Pray that you may not enter into temptation.' And He withdrew from them a stone's throw." Luke 22:40

*For the Sake of His Sorrowful Passion,*
*Have Mercy on Us and on the Whole World.*

4. "Father, if it be possible, let this cup pass from Me; nevertheless, not as I will, but as You will." Mark 14:36

*For the Sake of His Sorrowful Passion,*
*Have Mercy on Us and on the Whole World.*

5. "And being in an agony He prayed more earnestly and His sweat became like great drops of Blood falling down on the ground." Luke 22:44

*For the Sake of His Sorrowful Passion,*
*Have Mercy on Us and on the Whole World.*

6. "And there appeared to Him an angel from heaven strengthening Him." Luke 22:43

*For the Sake of His Sorrowful Passion,*
*Have Mercy on Us and on the Whole World.*

7. "And when He rose from prayer, He came to the disciples and found them sleeping.... 'The spirit is indeed willing, but the flesh is weak.'" Matthew 26:40-41

*For the Sake of His Sorrowful Passion,*
*Have Mercy on Us and on the Whole World.*

8. "And while He was still speaking, there came a crowd, and Judas leading them. 'Judas, would you betray the Son of Man with a kiss?'" Luke 22:47-48

*For the Sake of His Sorrowful Passion,*

*Have Mercy on Us and on the Whole World.*

9. "Put your sword back into its place; for all who take the sword will perish by the sword." Matthew 26:52

*For the Sake of His Sorrowful Passion,*
*Have Mercy on Us and on the Whole World.*

10. "Then all his disciples abandoned Him and fled.... Those who had seized Jesus led Him to Caiaphas the high priest...but Peter followed Him as far as the courtyard." Matthew 26:56-58

*For the Sake of His Sorrowful Passion,*
*Have Mercy on Us and on the Whole World.*

**The Scourging at the Pillar**

*Eternal Father, I Offer You the Body and Blood, Soul and Divinity of Your Dearly Beloved Son, Our Lord Jesus Christ, in Atonement for Our Sins and Those of the Whole World.*

1. "...the high priest asked Him: 'Are you the Christ, the Son of the Blessed One'.... And Jesus said: 'I am; and you will see the Son of Man sitting at the right hand of Power....'" Mark 14:61-62

*For the Sake of His Sorrowful Passion,*
*Have Mercy on Us and on the Whole World.*

2. "And they all condemned Him as deserving death. And some began to spit on Him and to strike Him...." Mark 14:64-65

*For the Sake of His Sorrowful Passion,*
*Have Mercy on Us and on the Whole World.*

3. "And as soon as it was morning, the chief priest, with the elders and scribes, and the whole council...led Him

away to Pilate." Mark 15:1

*For the Sake of His Sorrowful Passion,*
*Have Mercy on Us and on the Whole World.*

4. "We found this man…saying that He Himself is Christ a king." Luke 23:2

*For the Sake of His Sorrowful Passion,*
*Have Mercy on Us and on the Whole World.*

5. "Pilate…said: 'I do not find this man guilty of any of your charges against Him; neither did Herod…. I will therefore chastise Him and release Him.' But they all cried… 'Release to us Barabbas.'" Luke 23:14-18

*For the Sake of His Sorrowful Passion,*
*Have Mercy on Us and on the Whole World.*

6. "Pilate, wishing to satisfy the crowd, released for them Barabbas; and having Jesus scourged, gave Him over to their will." Mark 15:15

*For the Sake of His Sorrowful Passion,*
*Have Mercy on Us and on the Whole World.*

7. "I offered My back to those who struck Me." Isaiah 50:6

*For the Sake of His Sorrowful Passion,*
*Have Mercy on Us and on the Whole World.*

8. "The plowers plowed upon My back; they made their furrows long." Psalm 129:3

*For the Sake of His Sorrowful Passion,*
*Have Mercy on Us and on the Whole World.*

9. "He was wounded for our iniquities, He was bruised for our sins…and by His stripes we are healed." Isaiah 53:5

*For the Sake of His Sorrowful Passion,*

*Have Mercy on Us and on the Whole World.*

10. "Despised and the most abject of men, a man of sorrows and acquainted with infirmity." Isaiah 53:3

*For the Sake of His Sorrowful Passion,*
*Have Mercy on Us and on the Whole World.*

**The Crowning with Thorns**

*Eternal Father, I Offer You the Body and Blood, Soul and Divinity of Your Dearly Beloved Son, Our Lord Jesus Christ, in Atonement for Our Sins and Those of the Whole World.*

1. "Then the soldiers of the governor took Jesus into the praetorium and they gathered the whole battalion before Him." Matthew 27:27

*For the Sake of His Sorrowful Passion,*
*Have Mercy on Us and on the Whole World.*

2. "And they stripped Him and put a scarlet robe upon Him...." Matthew 27:28

*For the Sake of His Sorrowful Passion,*
*Have Mercy on Us and on the Whole World.*

3. "...and plaiting a crown of thorns, they put it on His Head...and they put a reed in His right Hand." Matthew 27:29

*For the Sake of His Sorrowful Passion,*
*Have Mercy on Us and on the Whole World.*

4. "And kneeling before Him they mocked Him saying: 'Hail, King of the Jews!' And they spat upon Him, and took the reed and struck Him on the Head." Matthew 27:29

*For the Sake of His Sorrowful Passion,*
*Have Mercy on Us and on the Whole World.*

5. "Pilate said: 'I am bringing Him out to you that you

may know that I find no crime in Him.'" John 19:4

*For the Sake of His Sorrowful Passion,*
*Have Mercy on Us and on the Whole World.*

6. "So Jesus came out, wearing the crown of thorns and the purple robe." John 19:5

*For the Sake of His Sorrowful Passion,*
*Have Mercy on Us and on the Whole World.*

7. "Pilate said, 'Behold the Man!'....but they cried out: 'Crucify Him, Crucify Him!'" John 19:5-6

*For the Sake of His Sorrowful Passion,*
*Have Mercy on Us and on the Whole World.*

8. "Pilate said, 'Shall I crucify your king?' ...the chief priests said: 'We have no king but Caesar.'" John 19:14-15

*For the Sake of His Sorrowful Passion,*
*Have Mercy on Us and on the Whole World.*

9. "And when they had mocked Him, they stripped Him of the robe, and put His own clothes on Him." Matthew 27:31

*For the Sake of His Sorrowful Passion,*
*Have Mercy on Us and on the Whole World.*

10. "Then he handed Him over to them to be crucified." John 19:16

*For the Sake of His Sorrowful Passion,*
*Have Mercy on Us and on the Whole World.*

**The Carrying of the Cross**

*Eternal Father, I Offer You the Body and Blood, Soul and Divinity of Your Dearly Beloved Son, Our Lord Jesus Christ, in Atonement for Our Sins and Those of the Whole World.*

1. "And (they) led Him away to crucify Him." Matthew 27:31

*For the Sake of His Sorrowful Passion,*
*Have Mercy on Us and on the Whole World.*

2. "...and He went out, bearing His own cross." John 19:17

*For the Sake of His Sorrowful Passion,*
*Have Mercy on Us and on the Whole World.*

3. "He has borne our infirmities." Isaiah 53:4

*For the Sake of His Sorrowful Passion,*
*Have Mercy on Us and on the Whole World.*

4. "And there followed Him a great multitude of the people and of women who bewailed and lamented Him. 'Daughters of Jerusalem, weep not for Me, but weep for yourselves and for your children.'" Luke 23:27-28

*For the Sake of His Sorrowful Passion,*
*Have Mercy on Us and on the Whole World.*

5. "...they seized one Simon of Cyrene, who was coming in from the country, and laid on him the cross, to carry it behind Jesus." Luke 23:26

*For the Sake of His Sorrowful Passion,*
*Have Mercy on Us and on the Whole World.*

6. "One who does not take up his cross and follow Me is not worthy of Me." Matthew 10:35

*For the Sake of His Sorrowful Passion,*
*Have Mercy on Us and on the Whole World.*

7. "He who puts his hand to the plow and turns back is not fit to be My disciple." Luke 9:62

*For the Sake of His Sorrowful Passion,*
*Have Mercy on Us and on the Whole World.*

8. “Like a lamb He was led to the slaughter and He opened not His mouth.” Isaiah 53:7

*For the Sake of His Sorrowful Passion,*
*Have Mercy on Us and on the Whole World.*

9. “And they brought Him to the place called Golgotha, which means the place of the skull.” Mark 15:22

*For the Sake of His Sorrowful Passion,*
*Have Mercy on Us and on the Whole World.*

10. “And they offered Him wine mingled with myrrh, but He would not drink it.” Mark 15:23

*For the Sake of His Sorrowful Passion,*
*Have Mercy on Us and on the Whole World.*

**The Crucifixion and Death of Jesus**

*Eternal Father, I Offer You the Body and Blood, Soul and Divinity of Your Dearly Beloved Son, Our Lord Jesus Christ, in Atonement for Our Sins and Those of the Whole World.*

1. “They have pieced My Hands and My Feet; they have numbered all My Bones.” Psalm 22:16

*For the Sake of His Sorrowful Passion,*
*Have Mercy on Us and on the Whole World.*

2. “They parted My garments among them and for My clothing they cast lots.” Psalm 22:18

*For the Sake of His Sorrowful Passion,*
*Have Mercy on Us and on the Whole World.*

3. “Jesus said: ‘Father, forgive them; for they know not what they do.’” Luke 23:34

*For the Sake of His Sorrowful Passion,*
*Have Mercy on Us and on the Whole World.*

4. "Jesus, remember me when You come into Your kingdom." And Jesus said to him: 'Amen, I say to you; this day you will be with Me in paradise.'" Luke 23:42-43

*For the Sake of His Sorrowful Passion,*
*Have Mercy on Us and on the Whole World.*

5. "...standing by the cross of Jesus was His Mother.... Jesus saw His Mother, and the disciple whom He loved standing near...." John 19:26

*For the Sake of His Sorrowful Passion,*
*Have Mercy on Us and on the Whole World.*

6. "He said to His mother: 'Woman, behold your son!' Then He said to the disciple: 'Behold, your mother!'" John 19:26-27

*For the Sake of His Sorrowful Passion,*
*Have Mercy on Us and on the Whole World.*

7. "At the ninth hour Jesus cried out with a loud voice: *'Eloi, Eloi, lama sabachthani?'* which means 'My God, my God, why have You forsaken me?'" Mark 15:34

*For the Sake of His Sorrowful Passion,*
*Have Mercy on Us and on the Whole World.*

8. "...Jesus, knowing that all was now finished, said to fulfill the scripture: 'I thirst.'" John 19:28

*For the Sake of His Sorrowful Passion,*
*Have Mercy on Us and on the Whole World.*

9. "Then Jesus, crying out with loud voice, said: 'Father, into Your hands I commend My spirit.'" Luke 23:46

*For the Sake of His Sorrowful Passion,*
*Have Mercy on Us and on the Whole World.*

10. "Jesus said, 'It is accomplished' and He bowed His

head and gave up His Spirit." John 19:30

*For the Sake of His Sorrowful Passion,*
*Have Mercy on Us and on the Whole World.*

## *Concluding Prayers for the Divine Mercy Chaplet*

1. Pray three times: "Holy God, Holy Mighty One, Holy Immortal One, have mercy on us and on the whole world."
2. Pray once: "Eternal God, in whom mercy is endless, and the treasury of compassion inexhaustible, look kindly upon us, and increase Your mercy in us, that in difficult moments, we might not despair, nor become despondent, but with great confidence, submit ourselves to Your holy will, which is Love and Mercy Itself. Amen."
3. With the crucifix, make the sign of the cross, while saying: "In the Name of the Father, and of the Son, and of the Holy Spirit. Amen."

# *The Franciscan Crown*
# *The Seven Joys of Mary*

The Franciscan Crown is variously known as the Seraphic Rosary or the Seven Joys of Mary. The historian, Friar Luke Waddy, places the origin of this devotion in its present form to 1422. He tells the story of a young Franciscan novice named James who as a child had been accustomed to offering Our Lady a crown of roses every day. When as a novice he was no longer able to perform this pious practice, James was moved to substitute seven decades of Hail Mary's as a "crown of spiritual roses".

While not contradicting the above explanation, other historians stress that these seven joyful mysteries of the Franciscan Crown developed gradually from the twelfth century. They were called *gaudes*, which urge Mary to "rejoice" in the favors God has granted her. Promotion of this devotion is attributed to such famous Franciscans as Saint Bonaventure, Saint John Capistran, and Saint Bernadine of Siena, among many others. It was also popular among other religious orders, such as the Cistercians and the Annunciades.

The popes have enriched this devotion of Mary's Seven Joys with many spiritual blessings. In fact, the Seraphic Rosary is one of very few rosaries where the blessings are not attached to the beads, but rather to the prayers and meditations themselves. Of course, beads of seven decades are very helpful in keeping track of one's prayers and are easily obtained from the Franciscans. But the traditional five-decade rosary can be used just as well. The paramount value of the Franciscan Crown lies in the fact that we, like Friar James, can daily offer Our Blessed Mother our own "crown of spiritual roses," one that is available in season and out...and never fades.

## *Pray the Franciscan Crown Using Rosary Beads and Scripture*

1. On the crucifix, make the sign of the cross, while saying: "In the Name of the Father, and of the Son and of the Holy Spirit. Amen."
2. Optional prayers can be added, similar to the regular (Dominican) Rosary, include the Apostles' Creed on the Crucifix, the Our Father on the first bead of the pendant, three Hail Mary's on the next three beads, and then the Glory Be. Or you can just go directly to the first decade.
3. On the first bead for each of the seven decades, announce the name of the Mystery and pray the Our Father.
4. Then, aloud or silently, read one verse from Scripture and pray one Hail Mary on each bead, as follows.

*(Note: The "Glory be" is not required at the end of each decade, but you may choose the option to pray it.)*

**The Annunciation**
*Our Father*

1. "...the angel Gabriel was sent from God to a city of Galilee named Nazareth...." Luke 1:26

*Hail Mary*

2. "...to a virgin betrothed to a man whose name was

Joseph of the house of David, and the virgin's name was Mary." Luke 1:27

*Hail Mary*

3. "Hail full of grace! The Lord is with you." Luke 1:28
*Hail Mary*

4. "Do not be afraid, Mary. You have found favor with God." Luke 1:30

*Hail Mary*

5. "Behold, you will conceive in your womb and bear a Son, and you shall call His name Jesus." Luke 1:31
*Hail Mary*

6. "Mary said to the angel: 'How can this be since I know not man?'" Luke 1:34

*Hail Mary*

7. "The Holy Spirit will come upon you and the power of the Most High will overshadow you...therefore, the Child to be born will be called Holy, the Son of God." Luke 1:35
*Hail Mary*

8. "Behold your kinswoman Elizabeth in her old age has also conceived a son.... For with God nothing is impossible." Luke 1:36

*Hail Mary*

9. "And Mary said: 'Behold the handmaid of the Lord. Be it done unto me according to your word.'" Luke 1:38
*Hail Mary*

10. "And the Word was made flesh and dwelt among us." John 1:14

*Hail Mary*

**The Visitation**
*Our Father*

1. "Mary...went with haste...entered the house of Zachariah and greeted Elizabeth...." Luke 1:39-40
*Hail Mary*

2. "The babe in her womb leaped and Elizabeth was filled with the Holy Spirit...." Luke 1:41
*Hail Mary*

3. "...blessed are you among women and blessed is the fruit of your womb...." Luke 1:42
*Hail Mary*

4. "...why is this granted to me that the mother of my Lord should come to me?" Luke 1:43
*Hail Mary*

5. "For behold when the sound of your greeting came to my ears, the babe in my womb leaped for joy." Luke 1:44
*Hail Mary*

6. "...and blessed is she who believed that what was spoken to her from the Lord would be fulfilled." Luke 1:45
*Hail Mary*

7. "And Mary said: 'My soul magnifies the Lord and my spirit rejoices in God my Savior....'" Luke 1:46-47
*Hail Mary*

8. "For He has regarded the lowliness of His handmaiden." Luke 1:48

*Hail Mary*

9. "For behold henceforth all generations will call me blessed...." Luke 1:48

*Hail Mary*

10. "...for He who is mighty has done great things for me, and holy is His name." Luke 1:49

*Hail Mary*

**The Nativity**

*Our Father*

1. "For behold a virgin shall conceive and bear a son and His name shall be called 'Emanuel', which means 'God with us'...." Matthew 1:23

*Hail Mary*

2. "A decree went out from Caesar Augustus...and Joseph went...to the city of David which is called Bethlehem...." Luke 2:1, 4

*Hail Mary*

3. "...Mary...gave birth to her firstborn Son and wrapped Him in swaddling clothes and laid Him in a manger, because there was no room for them in the inn." Luke 2:7

*Hail Mary*

4. "...an angel of the Lord appeared to the shepherds saying: '...I bring good news of great joy...for to you is born this day in the city of David a Savior, who is Christ the Lord...." Luke 2:9-10

*Hail Mary*

5. "Glory to God in the highest, and on earth peace to men of good will." Luke 2:14

*Hail Mary*

6. "And they went with haste and found Mary and Joseph and the Babe lying in a manger." Luke 2:16

*Hail Mary*

7. "They made known the saying which had been told them about this Child...and all who heard it wondered at what the shepherds told them." Luke 2:17-18

*Hail Mary*

8. "But Mary kept all these things, pondering them in her heart." Luke 2:19

*Hail Mary*

9. "And at the end of eight days, when He was circumcised, He was called Jesus...." Luke 2:21

*Hail Mary*

10. Mary and Joseph "brought Him to Jerusalem to present Him to the Lord." Luke 2:22

*Hail Mary*

**The Adoration of the Magi**

*Our Father*

1. "...behold wise men from the East came...saying: 'Where is He who has been born king of the Jews?'" Matthew 2:1-2

*Hail Mary*

2. "For we have seen His star in the East and have come to worship Him.'" Matthew 2:2

*Hail Mary*

3. "...Herod...assembling the priests and scribes...inquired of them where the Christ was to be born." Matthew 2:3-4

*Hail Mary*

4. "They told him: 'In Bethlehem of Judea, for so it is written by the prophet....'" Matthew 2:5

*Hail Mary*

5. "And you, Bethlehem, are by no means least...for from you shall come the ruler who will govern my people Israel." Micah 5:2

*Hail Mary*

6. "Then Herod...ascertained from them what time the star had appeared to them and he sent them to Bethlehem." Matthew 2:7-8

*Hail Mary*

7. "The star...went before them until it came to rest on the place where the Child was." Matthew 2:9

*Hail Mary*

8. "When they saw the star, they rejoiced exceedingly with great joy." Matthew 2:10

*Hail Mary*

9. "...they saw the Child with Mary His mother, and they fell down and worshiped Him." Matthew 2:11

*Hail Mary*

10. "...they offered him gifts of gold, frankincense and myrrh." Matthew 2:11

*Hail Mary*

**The Finding of the Child Jesus in the Temple**

*Our Father*

1. "Now His parents went up to Jerusalem every year at the feast of the Passover." Luke 2:41

*Hail Mary*

2. "And when He was twelve years old, they went up as was their custom." Luke 2:42

*Hail Mary*

3. "And when the feast was ended, as they were returning, the Boy Jesus stayed behind in Jerusalem. His parents did not know it." Luke 2:43

*Hail Mary*

4. "...but supposing Him to be in the company, they went a day's journey and they sought Him among their kinsfolk and acquaintances...." Luke 2:44

*Hail Mary*

5. " ...and when they did not find Him, they returned to Jerusalem seeking Him." Luke 2:45

*Hail Mary*

6. "After three days they found Him in the Temple, sitting among the teachers, listening to them and asking them questions. And all who heard Him were amazed at His understanding and His answers." Luke 2:46-47

*Hail Mary*

7. "And His mother said to Him: 'Son, why have you done so....Behold, Your father and I have been looking for You in sorrow.'" Luke 2:48

*Hail Mary*

8. "How is it that you sought Me? Did you not know that I must be about My Father's business?" Luke 2:49

*Hail Mary*

9. "And they did not understand the saying which He

spoke to them.... His mother kept all these things in her heart." Luke 2:50-51

*Hail Mary*

10. "And He went down to Nazareth and was obedient to them. And Jesus increased in wisdom and in stature and in favor with God and man." Luke 2:51-52

*Hail Mary*

**The Resurrection**

*Our Father*

1. "And when the Sabbath was over, Mary Magdalene, and Mary the mother of James, and Salome, brought spices.... Very early on the first day of the week they went to the tomb when the sun had risen." Mark 16:1-2

*Hail Mary*

2. "And looking up they saw that the stone was rolled back, for it was very large. And entering the tomb, they saw a young man...and they were amazed...." Mark 16:4

*Hail Mary*

3. "Do not be afraid! You seek Jesus of Nazareth, who was crucified. He has risen; He is not here.... But go tell His disciples and Peter...." Mark 16:6-7

*Hail Mary*

4. "Why do you seek the living among the dead? Remember how He told you: '...the Son of Man must be... crucified and on the third day rise.' And they remembered His words." Luke 24:5-8

*Hail Mary*

5. "The women told this to the Apostles, but…they didn't believe them." Luke 24:10-11

*Hail Mary*

6. "Mary…go to My brethren and say to them: 'I am ascending to My Father and your Father, to My God and your God.'" John 20:17

*Hail Mary*

7. "That very day two disciples were going to a village named Emmaus…. Jesus Himself drew near…but their eyes were kept from recognizing Him." Luke 24:13, 15-16

*Hail Mary*

8. "…we had hoped that He was the one to redeem Israel…. Moreover, some women of our company…had a vision of angels who said that He was alive." Luke 24:21-22

*Hail Mary*

9. "'Stay with us for it is getting toward evening and the day is now far spent.' So He went in to stay with them." Luke 24:29

*Hail Mary*

10. "When He was at table with them, He took bread and blessed and broke it…and their eyes were opened and they recognized Him…in the breaking of the bread." Luke 24:30-31

*Hail Mary*

**The Assumption and Coronation of Mary**

*Our Father*

1. "The Lord said to the Serpent: 'I will put enmities between you and the Woman and between your offspring

and her Offspring. He will crush your head and you will lie in wait for His heel.'" Genesis 3:15

*Hail Mary*

2. "My soul magnifies the Lord and my spirit rejoices in God my Savior; for He has regarded the lowliness of His handmaiden...." Luke 1:46-48

*Hail Mary*

3. "For behold, henceforth all generations shall call me blessed. For He who is mighty has done great things for me, and holy is His name." Luke 1:48-49

*Hail Mary*

4. "And a great sign appeared in heaven: a woman clothed with the sun, with the moon under her feet, and on her head a crown of twelve stars...." Revelation 12:1

*Hail Mary*

5. "...she was with Child and she cried out in her travail of birth, in anguish for delivery." Revelation 12:2

*Hail Mary*

6. "And another sign appeared in heaven: a great red dragon...." Revelation 12:3

*Hail Mary*

7. "And the dragon stood before the woman, who was about to bear a Child, that he might devour her Child when she brought Him forth...." Revelation 12:4

*Hail Mary*

8. "She brought forth a male Child, one who is to rule all the nations with a rod of iron. But her Child was caught up to God and to His throne." Revelation 12:5

*Hail Mary*

9. "And the woman fled into the wilderness, where she has a place prepared by God...." Revelation 12:6

*Hail Mary*

10. "The Spirit and the Bride say: 'Come'.... And let him who hears say: 'Come.' Amen! Come Lord Jesus." Revelation 22:17, 20

*Hail Mary*

## *Conclusion of the Franciscan Crown*

1. Add two Hail Mary's for the last two years of Our Lady's earthly sojourn.
2. Conclude with an Our Father, Hail Mary and Glory Be for the intentions of our Holy Father, the Pope.

## *The Seven Sorrows of Mary (The Servite Chaplet)*

The Seven Sorrows of Mary, or the Servite Chaplet, is also known as the Seven Dolors Rosary or Seven Swords. The latter title is derived from the Prophecy of Simeon to Mary: "...and your own soul a sword shall pierce, that the thoughts of many hearts may be revealed" (Luke 2:35).

This devotion has been popularized by the Servite Fathers through the years, but it was in the early eighteenth century that Popes Benedict XIII and Clement XII really promoted this devotion. Its historical development, however, goes back centuries; you will not be surprised to learn the Franciscans, Dominicans and Servites appeared on the scene at times not far apart from one another.

Even more striking is the close relationship between the Seven Joys of Mary in the Franciscan Crown and her Seven Sorrows in the Servite Chaplet. Notice how frequently the Sorrows co-mingle with the Joys of Jesus and Mary. They are often "just the other side of the coin." The traditional (Dominican) Rosary also beautifully combines those joys and sorrows.

The unique format of the Servite Chaplet, in a very real sense, counterbalances that of the Franciscan Crown. Both consist of seven sets of prayers: the Seven Sorrows has sets of seven Special Prayers, while the Crown has seven sets of ten Hail Mary's. Also like the Franciscan Crown, the seven-decade beads of the Seven Sorrows are not essential to receive their spiritual blessings; however, these beads are helpful and easily obtained from the Servites. The makeup of the specific beads for the Servite Chaplet are as follows: the Pendant consists of a large medallion, one large bead and three smaller beads; the Circlet is comprised of seven smaller medallions depicting the mysteries, each followed by a set of seven beads.

However, it is very easy to use traditional rosary beads to say the Seven Sorrows chaplet. You merely announce each mystery, say an Our Father, skip the first three beads in each decade, say a Hail Mary on the last seven beads of each decade, say the special prayer for that mystery, and then go on to the next decade.

## *Pray the Seven Sorrows of Mary Using Rosary Beads and Scripture*

1. On the crucifix, make the sign of the cross, while saying: "In the Name of the Father, and of the Son and of the Holy Spirit. Amen"
2. On the first bead for each of the seven decades, announce the name of the Mystery and pray the Our Father.
3. Skip the first three beads on each decade. Then, aloud or silently, read one verse from Scripture and pray one Hail Mary on each of the seven last beads in each decade, as follows.
4. After the seventh Hail Mary in each decade, pray: "Sorrowful and Immaculate Heart of Mary, pray for us.

*(Note: The "Glory be" is not required at the end of each decade, but you may choose the option to pray it.)*

**The Prophecy of Simeon**

*Our Father*

1. "Mary and Joseph...brought Him up to Jerusalem to present Him to the Lord." Luke 2:22

*Hail Mary*

2. "Now there was a man in Jerusalem whose name was Simeon...and the Holy Spirit was upon him." Luke 2:25

*Hail Mary*

3. "And inspired by the Spirit...he took Him in his arms and blessed God...." Luke 2:27

*Hail Mary*

4. "Lord, now you may let Your servant depart in peace according to Your word...." Luke 2:29

*Hail Mary*

5. "...for my eyes have seen Your salvation...a light of revelation to the Gentiles and glory to Your people Israel." Luke 2:30-32

*Hail Mary*

6. "Simeon blessed them and said to Mary, His mother: 'Behold this Child is set for the fall and rising of many in Israel and for a sign that will be contradicted....'" Luke 2:34

*Hail Mary*

7. "...and a sword will pierce through your own soul also, that the thoughts of many hearts may be revealed." Luke 2:35

*Hail Mary*

Pray once: "Sorrowful and Immaculate Heart of Mary, Pray for Us."

## The Flight into Egypt

*Our Father*

1. "...behold, wise men from the East came...saying: 'Where is He who has been born king of the Jews? For we have seen His star in the East and have come to worship Him.'" Matthew 2:1-2

*Hail Mary*

2. "Herod...ascertained from them what time the star had appeared and he sent them to Bethlehem.... 'Go and search diligently for the Child...and bring me word that I too may come and worship Him.'" Matthew 2:7-8

*Hail Mary*

3. "...they saw the Child with Mary His mother, and they fell down and worshiped Him.... They offered Him gifts of gold, frankincense and myrrh." Matthew 2:11

*Hail Mary*

4. "And being warned in a dream not to return to Herod, they departed to their own country by another way." Matthew 2:12

*Hail Mary*

5. "Behold, an angel of the Lord appeared to Joseph in a dream and said: Rise, take the Child and His Mother, and flee into Egypt...." Matthew 2:13

*Hail Mary*

6. "When Herod saw that he had been tricked by the wise men...he sent and killed all the male children...who were two years old or under, according to the time he had ascertained from the wise men." Matthew 2:16

*Hail Mary*

7. "Then was fulfilled what was spoken by the Prophet Jeremiah: 'A voice was heard in Ramah, wailing and loud lamentation, Rachel weeping for her children and refusing to be comforted for them, because they are no more.'" Jeremiah 31:15

*Hail Mary*

Pray once: "Sorrowful and Immaculate Heart of Mary, Pray for Us."

**The Loss of the Child Jesus in the Temple**

*Our Father*

1. "Now His parents went up to Jerusalem every year at the feast of the Passover. And when He was twelve years old, they went up as was their custom." Luke 2:41-42

*Hail Mary*

2. "And when the feast was ended, as they were returning, the Boy Jesus stayed behind in Jerusalem. His parents did not know it." Luke 2:43

*Hail Mary*

3. "...they went a day's journey and they sought Him among their kinsfolk and acquaintances and when they did not find Him, they returned to Jerusalem seeking Him." Luke 2:44-45

*Hail Mary*

4. "After three days they found Him in the Temple, sitting among the teachers, listening to them and asking them questions. And all who heard Him were amazed at His understanding and His answers." Luke 2:46-47

*Hail Mary*

5. "And His mother said to Him: 'Son, why have you done so.... Behold, Your father and I have been looking for You in sorrow.'" Luke 2:48

*Hail Mary*

6. "How is it that you sought Me? Did you not know that I must be about My Father's business?" Luke 2:49

*Hail Mary*

7. "And they did not understand the saying which He spoke to them ...(but) His mother kept all these things in her heart." Luke 2:50-51

*Hail Mary*

Pray once: "Sorrowful and Immaculate Heart of Mary, Pray for Us."

**The Meeting on the Way of the Cross**

*Our Father*

1. "...and He went out, bearing His own cross." John 19:17

*Hail Mary*

2. "He has borne our infirmities." Isaiah 53:4

*Hail Mary*

3. "And there followed Him a great multitude of the people and of women who bewailed and lamented Him. 'Daughters of Jerusalem, weep not for Me, but weep for yourselves and for your children.'" Luke 23:27-28

*Hail Mary*

4. "The soldiers...seized one Simon of Cyrene, who was coming in from the country, and laid on him the cross, to

carry it behind Jesus." Luke 23:26

*Hail Mary*

5. "One who does not take up his cross and follow Me is not worthy of Me." Matthew 10:38

*Hail Mary*

6. "Like a lamb He was led to the slaughter and He opened not His mouth." Isaiah 53:7

*Hail Mary*

7. "And they brought Him to the place called Golgotha, which means the place of the skull." Mark 15:22

*Hail Mary*

Pray once: "Sorrowful and Immaculate Heart of Mary, Pray for Us."

**The Crucifixion and Death of Jesus**

*Our Father*

1. "Jesus said: 'Father, forgive them; for they know not what they do.'" Luke 23:34

*Hail Mary*

2. "'Jesus, remember me when You come into Your kingdom.' And Jesus said to him: 'Amen, I say to you; this day you will be with Me in paradise.'" Luke 23:42-43

*Hail Mary*

3. "…standing by the cross of Jesus was His Mother…. Jesus saw His mother, and the disciple whom He loved standing near. He said to His mother: 'Woman, behold your son!' Then He said to the disciple: 'Behold, your mother!'" John 19:26-27

*Hail Mary*

4. "At the ninth hour Jesus cried out with a loud voice: *'Eloi, Eloi, lama sabachthani?'* which means: 'My God, my God, why have You forsaken me?'" Mark 15:34

*Hail Mary*

5. "...Jesus, knowing that all was now finished, said to fulfill the scripture: 'I thirst.'" John 19:28

*Hail Mary*

6. "Then Jesus, crying out with a loud voice, said: 'Father, into Your hands I commend My spirit.'" Luke 23:46

*Hail Mary*

7. "Jesus said, 'It is accomplished,' and He bowed His head and gave up His Spirit." John 19:30

*Hail Mary*

Pray once: "Sorrowful and Immaculate Heart of Mary, Pray for Us."

**The Body of Jesus Is Taken Down from the Cross**
*Our Father*

1. "...to prevent the bodies from remaining on the cross on the Sabbath...the Jews asked Pilate that their legs be broken and they be taken away." John 19:31

*Hail Mary*

2. "But when they came to Jesus and saw that He was already dead, they did not break His legs." John 19:33

*Hail Mary*

3. "But one of the soldiers pierced His side with a spear...." John 19:34

*Hail Mary*

4. “Not a bone of Him shall be broken....” Psalm 34:21

*Hail Mary*

5. “And Joseph of Arimathea...took courage and went to Pilate and asked for the Body of Jesus.” Mark 15:43

*Hail Mary*

6. “Nicodemus also, who had at first come to Him by night, came bringing a mixture of myrrh and aloes, about a hundred pounds weight....” John 19:39

*Hail Mary*

7. “Joseph bought a linen shroud and, taking Him down, they wrapped Him in the linen shroud....” Mark 15:46

*Hail Mary*

Pray once: “Sorrowful and Immaculate Heart of Mary, Pray for Us.”

**The Burial of Jesus’ Body**

*Our Father*

1. “Now in the place where He was crucified, there was a garden, and in the garden was a new tomb where no one had ever been buried.” John 19:41

*Hail Mary*

2. “Because of the Jewish day of Preparation, as the tomb was close at hand, they laid Jesus there.” John 19:42

*Hail Mary*

3. “Joseph placed the Body of Jesus in his own new tomb, which he had hewn in the rock.” Matthew 27:60

*Hail Mary*

4. "Joseph rolled a great stone to the door of the tomb, and departed." Matthew 27:60

*Hail Mary*

5. "The women...saw the tomb, and how the Body was laid; then they returned and prepared the spices and ointments." Luke 23:55-56

*Hail Mary*

6. "...the chief priests and the Pharisees gathered before Pilate. 'Sir, we remember how that Impostor said, while He was still alive: "After three days I will rise again."'" Matthew 27:62-63

*Hail Mary*

7. "Pilate said: 'You have a guard of soldiers; go, make it as secure as you can.' So they went and made the sepulcher secure by sealing the stone and setting a guard." Matthew 27:65-66

*Hail Mary*

Pray once: "Sorrowful and Immaculate Heart of Mary, Pray for Us."

## *Conclusion of the Seven Sorrows*

1. Pray once: "Pray for us, O most Sorrowful Virgin, that we may be made worthy of the promises of Christ."
2. Pray once: "Lord Jesus, we implore, both for the present and for the hour of our death, the intercession of the Most Blessed Virgin Mary, Thy Mother, whose soul was pierced by a sword of grief. Grant us this favor, O Savior of the world, Who lives and reigns with the Father and the Holy Spirit, forever and ever. Amen."
3. Say three Hail Mary's for the tears Mary shed.

## *The (Dominican) Rosary*

The title, "Dominican Rosary", may strike you as odd, because for centuries it has been best known to us simply as "The Rosary". But contrary to general opinion, this most popular of Marian devotions did not receive its more final form until the 1500s. Furthermore, in 2002 the great Pope John Paul II expanded the Rosary by adding five new Mysteries, called the Luminous Mysteries (also known as the Mysteries of Light). Thus, the Rosary now has twenty decades divided into four sets of mysteries: the Joyous, the Luminous, the Sorrowful and the Glorious. These truly represent the full History of Salvation, i.e.: the story of Jesus from His conception through His public life, His suffering and death, and culminating in His glorification (as well as that of His mother).

To bring us to this present fulfillment, the Rosary boasts hundreds of years of grass roots development, for it is truly a prayer that blossomed from the ordinary faithful. Especially in the Western Church, many scholars believe that this form of prayer arose from the effort of lay people to participate in the Divine Office of the priests, nuns and monks. Their Breviary consisted of praying the 150 Psalms in Latin. Many lay people, who could not read Latin, began substituting 150 Our Father's or Hail Mary's or a combination of both prayers, dividing them into 15 decades of ten prayers. Of course, the use of prayer beads or knots to keep track of the these prayers was nothing new. Beads exist among every major civilization, then and now.

The Rosary has been greatly enriched with spiritual blessings by countless popes down through the ages. But it is to the Church's spiritual sons and daughters of the great Saint Dominick that we should offer our deepest appreciation for popularizing the devotion we enjoy today. With the Rosary, we lay people can recall the full Mysteries of Christ in prayer and action.

Some people have the time to pray all twenty mysteries of the Rosary each day. In that case, the order is Joyous, Luminous, Sorrowful and Glorious. For most people, in order to pray all twenty mysteries each week, different mysteries are generally prayed on the following days of the week:

Joyful Mysteries on Mondays and Saturdays;
Luminous Mysteries on Thursdays;
Sorrowful Mysteries on Tuesdays and Fridays;
Glorious Mysteries on Wednesdays and Sundays.

## *Pray the (Dominican) Rosary Using Rosary Beads and Scripture*

1. On the crucifix, make the sign of the cross, while saying: "In the Name of the Father, and of the Son, and of the Holy Spirit. Amen."
2. Then pray The Apostles' Creed
3. On the first bead, pray the Our Father.
4. On the cluster of three beads, pray three Hail Marys.

*Option: It is a common practice to pray here for an increase in the three great cardinal virtues of Faith, Hope and Charity.*

5. After the Hail Marys, pray the Glory Be once.
6. On the first bead of each of the five mysteries, announce the name of the mystery and pray the Our Father.
7. Then, aloud or silently, read one verse from Scripture and then say a Hail Mary on each of the ten beads, as follows.

*Options at the end of each decade: Latin Americans often say: "O Sacrament Most Holy, O Sacrament Divine, all praise and all thanksgiving be every moment Thine." Croatians and those devoted to Medjugorje say: "Queen of Peace, pray for us." Portuguese and those devoted to Fatima say: "O My Jesus, forgive us our sins, save us from the fires of hell, lead all souls to Heaven, especially those most in need of Your Mercy."*

## *The Joyful Mysteries*

### The Annunciation

*Our Father*

1. "...the angel Gabriel was sent from God to a city of Galilee named Nazareth...." Luke 1:26

*Hail Mary*

2. "...to a virgin betrothed to a man whose name was Joseph of the house of David and the virgin's name was Mary." Luke 1:27

*Hail Mary*

3. "Hail full of grace! The Lord is with you." Luke 1:28

*Hail Mary*

4. "Do not be afraid, Mary. You have found favor with God." Luke 1:30

*Hail Mary*

5. "Behold, you will conceive in your womb and bear a Son, and you shall call His name Jesus." Luke 1:31

*Hail Mary*

6. "Mary said to the angel: 'How can this be since I know not man?'" Luke 1:34

*Hail Mary*

7. "The Holy Spirit will come upon you and the power of the Most High will overshadow you...therefore, the Child to be born will be called Holy, the Son of God." Luke 1:35

*Hail Mary*

8. "Behold your kinswoman Elizabeth in her old age has also conceived a son.... For with God nothing is impossible." Luke 1:36

*Hail Mary*

9. "And Mary said: 'Behold the handmaid of the Lord. Be it done unto me according to your word.'" Luke 1:38

*Hail Mary*

10. "And the Word was made flesh and dwelt among us." John 1:14

*Hail Mary*

*Glory Be*

**The Visitation**

*Our Father*

1. "Mary...went with haste...entered the house of Zachariah and greeted Elizabeth...." Luke 1:39-40

*Hail Mary*

2. "The babe in her womb leaped and Elizabeth was filled with the Holy Spirit...." Luke 1:41

*Hail Mary*

3. "...blessed are you among women and blessed is the fruit of your womb...." Luke 1:42

*Hail Mary*

4. "...why is this granted to me that the mother of my

Lord should come to me?" Luke 1:43

*Hail Mary*

5. "For behold, when the sound of your greeting came to my ears, the babe in my womb leaped for joy." Luke 1:44

*Hail Mary*

6. "...and blessed is she who believed that what was spoken to her from the Lord would be fulfilled." Luke 1:45

*Hail Mary*

7. "And Mary said: 'My soul magnifies the Lord and my spirit rejoices in God my Savior....'" Luke 1:46-47

*Hail Mary*

8. "For He has regarded the lowliness of His handmaiden." Luke 1:48

*Hail Mary*

9. "For behold henceforth all generations will call me blessed...." Luke 1:48

*Hail Mary*

10. "...for He who is mighty has done great things for me, and holy is His name." Luke 1:49

*Hail Mary*

*Glory Be*

**The Nativity**

*Our Father*

1. "For behold a virgin shall conceive and bear a son and His name shall be called 'Emanuel', which means 'God with us.'" Matthew 1:23

*Hail Mary*

2. "And you, Bethlehem, are a little one among the towns of Judah; but out of you shall He come forth unto Me, Him who is to be the ruler in Israel." Micah 5:2

*Hail Mary*

3. "A decree went out from Caesar Augustus...and Joseph went ...to the city of David which is called Bethlehem...." Luke 2:1, 4

*Hail Mary*

4. "...Mary...gave birth to her firstborn Son and wrapped Him in swaddling clothes and laid Him in a manger, because there was no room for them in the inn." Luke 2:7

*Hail Mary*

5. "...an angel of the Lord appeared to the shepherds saying: '...I bring good news of great joy ...for to you is born this day in the city of David a Savior who is Christ the Lord....'" Luke 2:9-10

*Hail Mary*

6. "Glory to God in the highest, and on earth peace to men of good will." Luke 2:14

*Hail Mary*

7. "And they went with haste and found Mary and Joseph and the Babe lying in a manger. They made known the saying which had been told them about this Child." Luke 2:16-17

*Hail Mary*

8. "And all who heard it wondered at what the shepherds told them. But Mary kept all these things, pondering them in her heart." Luke 2:18-19

*Hail Mary*

9. "And the shepherds returned, glorifying and praising God for all they had heard and seen...." Luke 2:20

*Hail Mary*

10. "And at the end of eight days, when He was circumcised, He was called Jesus...." Luke 2:21

*Hail Mary*

*Glory Be*

**The Presentation in the Temple**

*Our Father*

1. "...they brought Him up to Jerusalem to present Him to the Lord." Luke 2:22

*Hail Mary*

2. "Now there was a man in Jerusalem whose name was Simeon...and the Holy Spirit was upon him." Luke 2:25

*Hail Mary*

3. "And it had been revealed to him that he should not see death before he had seen the Lord's Christ." Luke 2:26

*Hail Mary*

4. "And inspired by the Spirit...he took Him in his arms and blessed God...." Luke 2:27-28

*Hail Mary*

5. "Lord, now you may let Your servant depart in peace according to Your word...for my eyes have seen Your salvation ...a light of revelation to the Gentiles and glory to Your people Israel." Luke 2:29-32

*Hail Mary*

6. "Simeon blessed them and said to Mary His mother:

'Behold this Child is set for the fall and rising of many in Israel and for a sign that will be contradicted....'" Luke 2:34

*Hail Mary*

7. "...and a sword will pierce through your own soul also, that the thoughts of many hearts may be revealed." Luke 2:35

*Hail Mary*

8. "And there was a prophetess, Anna, who did not depart from the temple, worshiping with fasting and prayer day and night." Luke 2:36-37

*Hail Mary*

9. "And coming up at that very hour she gave thanks to God, and kept speaking of Him to all who were looking for the redemption of Israel." Luke 2:38

*Hail Mary*

10. "...behold wise men from the East came...saying: 'Where is He who has been born king of the Jews?'" Matthew 2:1-2

*Hail Mary*

*Glory Be*

**The Finding of the Child Jesus in the Temple**

*Our Father*

1. "Now His parents went up to Jerusalem every year at the feast of the Passover." Luke 2:41

*Hail Mary*

2. "And when He was 12 years old, they went up as was their custom." Luke 2:42

*Hail Mary*

3. "And when the feast was ended, as they were returning, the Boy Jesus stayed behind in Jerusalem. His parents did not know it." Luke 2:43

*Hail Mary*

4. "...but supposing Him to be in the company, they went a day's journey and they sought Him among their kinsfolk and acquaintances...." Luke 2:44

*Hail Mary*

5. " ...and when they did not find Him, they returned to Jerusalem seeking Him." Luke 2:45

*Hail Mary*

6. "After three days they found Him in the Temple, sitting among the teachers, listening to them and asking them questions. And all who heard Him were amazed at His understanding and His answers." Luke 2:46-47

*Hail Mary*

7. "And His mother said to Him: 'Son, why have you done so.... Behold, Your father and I have been looking for You in sorrow.'" Luke 2:48

*Hail Mary*

8. "How is it that you sought Me? Did you not know that I must be about My Father's business?" Luke 2:49

*Hail Mary*

9. "And they did not understand the saying which He spoke to them.... His mother kept all these things in her heart." Luke 2:50-51

*Hail Mary*

10. "He went down to Nazareth and was obedient to them. And Jesus increased in wisdom and in stature and in favor with God and man." Luke 2:51-52

*Hail Mary*

*Glory Be*

**Prayers after the Joyful Mysteries (Unless All Twenty Decades of the Rosary Are Being Said at Once)**

1. Pray the Hail Holy Queen.
2. "Let us pray: O God - Whose Only Begotten Son by His Life, Death and Resurrection has purchased for us the rewards of eternal life – grant, we beseech You, that meditating on these Mysteries of the most holy Rosary of the Blessed Virgin Mary, we may imitate what they contain and obtain what they promise, through the same Christ our Lord. Amen."
3. Pray one Our Father, one Hail Mary and one Glory Be for the intention of the Holy Father.
4. Options:
   a. "May the Divine Assistance remain always with us. And may the souls of the faithful departed, through the mercy of God, rest in peace. Amen."
   b. "May the Sacred Heart of Jesus, in the Most Blessed Sacrament of the Altar, be praised adored and loved, with grateful affection, at every moment, in all the tabernacles of the world, even to the end of time. Amen."
   c. "St. Michael the Archangel, defend us in battle. Be our safeguard against the wickedness and snares of the devil. Rebuke him, O God, we humbly pray and do you, O Prince of the Heavenly Hosts, by the power

of God, cast into hell Satan and all the evil spirits who roam about the world seeking the ruin of souls. Amen."

5. On the crucifix, make the Sign of the Cross, while praying: "In the Name of the Father, and of the Son, and of the Holy Spirit. Amen."

## *The Luminous Mysteries*

### The Baptism of Jesus

*Our Father*

1. "In those days came John the Baptist preaching: ... 'Repent, for the kingdom of heaven is at hand.'"Matthew 3:1-2

*Hail Mary*

2. "The voice of one crying in the wilderness: Prepare the way of the Lord, make straight His paths." Isaiah 40:3-4

*Hail Mary*

3. "They went out to him...and were baptized by him in the river Jordan, confessing their sins." Matthew 3:5-6

*Hail Mary*

4, "Then Jesus came...to John, to be baptized by him." Matthew 3:13

*Hail Mary*

5. "John would have prevented Him, saying: 'I need to be baptized by You, and do You come to me?'" Matthew 3:14

*Hail Mary*

6. "And when Jesus was baptized...behold the heavens

were opened and he saw the Spirit of God descending like a dove and resting on Him...." Matthew 3:16

*Hail Mary*

7. "...and lo, a voice from heaven, saying: 'This is My beloved Son, with whom I am well pleased.'" Matthew 3:17

*Hail Mary*

8. "The next day John saw Jesus coming toward him and said: 'Behold the Lamb of God, who takes away the sin of the world.'" John 1:29

*Hail Mary*

9. "This is He who baptizes with the Holy Spirit. And I have seen this and borne witness that this is the Son of God." John 1:34

*Hail Mary*

10. "Then Jesus was led by the Spirit into the wilderness to be tempted by the devil." Matthew 4:1

*Hail Mary*

*Glory Be*

**The Miracle at the Marriage Feast in Cana**

*Our Father*

1. "...there was a marriage at Cana in Galilee, and the mother of Jesus was there...." John 2:1

*Hail Mary*

2. "Jesus also was invited to the marriage along with his disciples." John 2:2

*Hail Mary*

3. "When the wine failed, the mother of Jesus said to Him: 'They have no wine.'" John 2:3

*Hail Mary*

4. "And Jesus said to her: 'What is that to you and to Me? My hour has not yet come.'" John 2:4

*Hail Mary*

5. "His mother said to the servants: 'Do whatever He tells you.'" John 2:5

*Hail Mary*

6. "Jesus said to them: 'Fill the jars with water.' And they filled them to the brim." John 2:7

*Hail Mary*

7. "Now draw some out, and take it to the steward of the feast." John 2:8

*Hail Mary*

8. "When the steward of the feast tasted the water now become wine...he called the bridegroom...." John 2:9

*Hail Mary*

9. "Everyone serves the good wine first and...then the poor wine; but you have kept the good wine until now." John 2:10

*Hail Mary*

10. "This, the first of His signs, Jesus did at Cana in Galilee, and manifested His glory; and His disciples believed in Him." John 2:11

*Hail Mary*

*Glory Be*

**The Proclamation of the Kingdom**

*Our Father*

1. "And He went about all Galilee, teaching in their synagogues and preaching the gospel of the kingdom...." Matthew 4:23

*Hail Mary*

2. "The Lord your God is one: you shall love the Lord your God with your whole heart....and you shall love your neighbor as yourself." Mark 12:29

*Hail Mary*

3. "Think not that I have come to abolish the Law and the Prophets...rather I have come to fulfill them." Matthew 5:17

*Hail Mary*

4. "Do unto to others as you would have them do unto you: for this is the Law and the Prophets." Matthew 7:12

*Hail Mary*

5. "A new commandment I give to you, that you love one another as I have loved you.... By this will all men know that you are My disciples." John 13:34

*Hail Mary*

6. "Love your enemies and pray for those who persecute you." Matthew 5:44

*Hail Mary*

7. "Seeing the crowds, He went up on the mountain and he sat down...and taught them, saying: 'Blessed are the poor in spirit, for theirs is the kingdom of heaven....'" Matthew 5:1-4

*Hail Mary*

8. "Blessed are those that mourn....meek....thirst for righteousness....merciful....pure in heart....peacemakers...." Matthew 5:5-10

*Hail Mary*

9. "You are the salt of the earth.... You are the light of the world." Matthew 5:22

*Hail Mary*

10. "Greater love than this no man has: that a man lay day his life for his friends." John 15:3

*Hail Mary*

*Glory Be*

**The Transfiguration**

*Our Father*

1. "...Jesus took with Him Peter, James and John his brother, and led them up a high mountain apart." Matthew 17:1

*Hail Mary*

2. "And He was transfigured before them, and His face shone like the sun, and His garments became white as light." Matthew 17:2

*Hail Mary*

3. "And behold, two men talked with Him, Moses and Elijah, who appeared in glory and spoke of His departure." Luke 9:31-31

*Hail Mary*

4. "And Peter said to Jesus: 'Master, it is good that we are

here; Let us make three booths: one for You, one for Moses and one for Elijah....'" Mark 9:5

*Hail Mary*

5. "He was still speaking when behold a bright cloud overshadowed them...." Matthew 17:5

*Hail Mary*

6. "This is My beloved Son, with whom I am well pleased; listen to Him." 2 Peter 1:17

*Hail Mary*

7. "When the disciples heard this, they fell on their faces, and were filled with fear." Matthew 17:6

*Hail Mary*

8. "But Jesus came and touched them, saying: 'Rise and have no fear.'" Matthew 17:7

*Hail Mary*

9. "And when they lifted up their eyes, they saw no one, but only Jesus." Matthew 17:8

*Hail Mary*

10. "As they were coming down the mountain, Jesus commanded them: 'Tell no one the vision, until the Son of Man is raised from the dead.'" Matthew 17:9

*Hail Mary*

*Glory Be*

**The Institution of the Eucharist**

*Our Father*

1. "...He sat down at table, and the disciples with Him. And He said to them: 'I have earnestly desired to eat this

Passover with you before I suffer.'" Luke 2:15

*Hail Mary*

2. "And during the supper…Jesus laid aside his garments, and…began to wash the disciples' feet." John 13:2, 4-5

*Hail Mary*

3. "If I, then, your Lord and Master, have washed your feet, you also ought to wash one another's feet." John 13:14

*Hail Mary*

4. "One of you will betray Me…." "Is it I, Lord?" Mark 14:18-19

*Hail Mary*

5. "…Jesus took bread, blessed and broke it, and gave it to the disciples and said: 'Take and eat; this is My Body.'" Matthew 26:26

*Hail Mary*

6. "And He took a cup, and when He had given thanks, He gave it to them, saying: 'Drink of it all of you, for this is My Blood of the New Covenant. Do this in memory of Me.'" Matthew 26:27-28

*Hail Mary*

7. "For as often as you eat this Bread and drink this Cup, you proclaim the Death of the Lord until He comes." 2 Corinthians 11:26

*Hail Mary*

8. "Amen, Amen, I say to you, unless you eat the Flesh of the Son of Man and drink His Blood, you have no life in you." John 5:53

*Hail Mary*

9. "He who eats My Flesh and drinks My Blood abides in Me and I in him. And I will raise him up on the last day." John 6:56

*Hail Mary*

10. "The Cup of blessing which we bless, is it not a participation in the Blood of Christ? The Bread which we break, is it not a participation in the Body of Christ?" 1 Corinthians 10:16, 17

*Hail Mary*

*Glory Be*

**Prayers after the Luminous Mysteries (Unless All Twenty Decades of the Rosary Are Being Said at Once)**

1. Pray the Hail Holy Queen.
2. "Let us pray: O God - Whose Only Begotten Son by His Life, Death and Resurrection has purchased for us the rewards of eternal life – grant, we beseech You, that meditating on these Mysteries of the most holy Rosary of the Blessed Virgin Mary, we may imitate what they contain and obtain what they promise, through the same Christ our Lord. Amen."
3. Pray one Our Father, one Hail Mary and one Glory Be for the intention of the Holy Father.
4. Options:
   a. "May the Divine Assistance remain always with us. And may the souls of the faithful departed, through the mercy of God, rest in peace. Amen."
   b. "May the Sacred Heart of Jesus, in the Most Blessed Sacrament of the Altar, be praised adored and loved, with grateful affection, at every moment, in all the tabernacles of the world, even to the end of time. Amen."

c. "St. Michael the Archangel, defend us in battle. Be our safeguard against the wickedness and snares of the devil. Rebuke him, O God, we humbly pray and do you, O Prince of the Heavenly Hosts, by the power of God, cast into hell Satan and all the evil spirits who roam about the world seeking the ruin of souls. Amen."

5. On the crucifix, make the Sign of the Cross, while praying: "In the Name of the Father, and of the Son, and of the Holy Spirit. Amen."

## *The Sorrowful Mysteries*

### The Agony in the Garden

*Our Father*

1. "And they went to a Place which was called Gethsemane; and He said to his disciples: 'Sit here while I pray.'" Mark 14:32

*Hail Mary*

2. "And He took with Him Peter, James and John and began to be greatly distressed and troubled. 'My soul is sorrowful, even unto death.'" Mark 14:33-34

*Hail Mary*

3. "(Jesus said), 'Pray that you may not enter into temptation.' And He withdrew from them a stone's throw." Luke 22:40

*Hail Mary*

4. "Father, if it be possible, let this cup pass from Me; nevertheless, not as I will, but as You will." Mark 14:36

*Hail Mary*

5. "And being in an agony He prayed more earnestly and

His sweat became like great drops of Blood falling down on the ground." Luke 22:44

*Hail Mary*

6. "And there appeared to Him an angel from heaven strengthening Him." Luke 22:43

*Hail Mary*

7. "...He came to the disciples and found them sleeping.... 'The spirit is indeed willing, but the flesh is weak.'" Matthew 26:40-41

*Hail Mary*

8. "And while He was still speaking, then came a crowd and with Judas leading them: 'Judas, would you betray the Son of Man with a kiss?'" Luke 22:47-48

*Hail Mary*

9. "Put your sword back into its place; for all who take the sword will perish by the sword." Matthew 26:52

*Hail Mary*

10. "Then all his disciples abandoned Him and fled.... Those who had seized Jesus led Him to Caiaphas the high priest...but Peter followed Him as far as the courtyard." Matthew 26:56-58

*Hail Mary*

*Glory Be*

**The Scourging at the Pillar**

*Our Father*

1. "...the high priest asked Him: 'Are you the Christ, the Son of the Blessed One'....And Jesus said: 'I am; and you

will see the Son of Man sitting at the right hand of Power....'" Mark 14:61-62

*Hail Mary*

2. "And they all condemned Him as deserving death. And some began to spit on Him and to strike Him...." Mark 14:64-65

*Hail Mary*

3. "And as soon as it was morning, the chief priest, with the elders and scribes, and the whole council...led Him away to Pilate." Mark 15:1

*Hail Mary*

4. "We found this man...saying that He Himself is Christ a king." Luke 23:2

*Hail Mary*

5. "Pilate...said: 'I do not find this man guilty of any of your charges against Him; neither did Herod.... I will therefore chastise Him and release Him.' But they all cried... 'Release to us Barabbas.'" Luke 23:14-18

*Hail Mary*

6. "Pilate, wishing to satisfy the crowd, released for them Barabbas; and having Jesus scourged, gave Him over to their will." Mark 15:15

*Hail Mary*

7. "I offered My back to those who struck Me." Isaiah 50:6

*Hail Mary*

8. "The plowers plowed upon My back; they made their furrows long." Psalm 129:3

*Hail Mary*

9. "He was wounded for our iniquities, He was bruised for our sins...and by His stripes we are healed." Isaiah 53:5

*Hail Mary*

10. "Despised and the most abject of men, a man of sorrows and acquainted with infirmity." Isaiah 53:3

*Hail Mary*

*Glory Be*

**The Crowning with Thorns**

*Our Father*

1. "Then the soldiers of the governor took Jesus into the praetorium and they gathered the whole battalion before Him." Matthew 27:27

*Hail Mary*

2. "And they stripped Him and put a scarlet robe upon Him...." Matthew 27:28

*Hail Mary*

3. "...and plaiting a crown of thorns, they put it on His Head...and they put a reed in His right hand." Matthew 27:29

*Hail Mary*

4. "And kneeling before Him they mocked Him saying: 'Hail, King of the Jews!' And they spat upon Him, and took the reed and struck Him on the Head." Matthew 27:29

*Hail Mary*

5. "Pilate said: 'I am bringing Him out to you that you may know that I find no crime in Him.'" John 19:4

*Hail Mary*

6. "So Jesus came out, wearing the crown of thorns and the purple robe." John 19:5

*Hail Mary*

7. "Pilate said, 'Behold the Man!' ...but they cried out: 'Crucify Him, Crucify Him!'" John 19:5-6

*Hail Mary*

8. "Pilate said, 'Shall I crucify your king?' ...the chief priests said: 'We have no king but Caesar.'" John 19:14-15

*Hail Mary*

9. "And when they had mocked Him, they stripped Him of the robe, and put His own clothes on Him." Matthew 27:31

*Hail Mary*

10. "Then he handed Him over to them to be crucified." John 19:16

*Hail Mary*

*Glory Be*

**The Carrying of the Cross**

*Our Father*

1. "And (they) led Him away to crucify Him." Matthew 27:31

*Hail Mary*

2. "...and He went out, bearing His own cross." John 19:17

*Hail Mary*

3. "He has borne our infirmities." Isaiah 53:4

*Hail Mary*

4. "And there followed Him a great multitude of the people and of women who bewailed and lamented Him. 'Daughters of Jerusalem, weep not for Me, but weep for yourselves and for your children.'" Luke 23:27-28

*Hail Mary*

5. "...they seized one Simon of Cyrene, who was coming in from the country, and laid on him the cross, to carry it behind Jesus." Luke 23:26

*Hail Mary*

6. "One who does not take up his cross and follow Me is not worth of Me." Matthew 10:38

*Hail Mary*

7. "He who puts his hand to the plow and turns back is not fit to be My disciple." Luke 9:62

*Hail Mary*

8. "Like a lamb He was led to the slaughter and He opened not His mouth." Isaiah 53:7

*Hail Mary*

9. "And they brought Him to the place called Golgotha, which means the place of the skull." Mark 15:22

*Hail Mary*

10. "And they offered Him wine mingled with myrrh, but He would not drink it." Mark 15:23

*Hail Mary*

*Glory Be*

### The Crucifixion and Death of Jesus

*Our Father*

1. "They pierced my hands and my feet; they have numbered all my bones." Psalm 22:16

*Hail Mary*

2. "They parted My garments among them and for My clothing they cast lots." Psalm 22:18

*Hail Mary*

3. "Jesus said: 'Father, forgive them; for they know not what they do.'" Luke 23:34

*Hail Mary*

4. "The thief said, 'Jesus, remember me when You come into Your kingdom.' And Jesus said to him: 'Amen, I say to you; this day you will be with Me in paradise.'" Luke 23:42-43

*Hail Mary*

5. "...standing by the cross of Jesus was His Mother.... Jesus saw His mother, and the disciple whom He loved standing near." John 19:26

*Hail Mary*

6. "He said to His mother: 'Woman, behold your son!' Then He said to the disciple: 'Behold, your mother!'" John 19:26-27

*Hail Mary*

7. "At the ninth hour Jesus cried with a loud voice: *'Eloi, Eloi, lama sabachthani?'* which means: 'My God, my God, why have You forsaken me?'" Mark 15:34

*Hail Mary*

8. "…Jesus, knowing that all was now finished, said to fulfill the scripture: 'I thirst.'" John 19:28

*Hail Mary*

9. "Then Jesus, crying with a loud voice, said: 'Father, into Your hands I commend My spirit.'" Luke 23:46

*Hail Mary*

10 "(Jesus said,) 'It is accomplished,' and He bowed His head and gave up His Spirit." John 19:30

*Hail Mary*

*Glory Be*

**Prayers after the Sorrowful Mysteries (Unless All Twenty Decades of the Rosary Are Being Said at Once)**

1. Pray the Hail Holy Queen.
2. "Let us pray: O God - Whose Only Begotten Son by His Life, Death and Resurrection has purchased for us the rewards of eternal life – grant, we beseech You, that meditating on these Mysteries of the most holy Rosary of the Blessed Virgin Mary, we may imitate what they contain and obtain what they promise, through the same Christ our Lord. Amen."
3. Pray one Our Father, one Hail Mary and one Glory Be for the intention of the Holy Father.
4. Options:
   a. "May the Divine Assistance remain always with us. And may the souls of the faithful departed, through the mercy of God, rest in peace. Amen."
   b. "May the Sacred Heart of Jesus, in the Most Blessed Sacrament of the Altar, be praised adored and loved, with grateful affection, at every moment, in all the tab-

ernacles of the world, even to the end of time. Amen."

c. "St. Michael the Archangel, defend us in battle. Be our safeguard against the wickedness and snares of the devil. Rebuke him, O God, we humbly pray and do you, O Prince of the Heavenly Hosts, by the power of God, cast into hell Satan and all the evil spirits who roam about the world seeking the ruin of souls. Amen."

5. On the crucifix, make the Sign of the Cross, while praying: "In the Name of the Father, and of the Son, and of the Holy Spirit. Amen."

## *The Glorious Mysteries*

### The Resurrection

*Our Father*

1. "Joseph of Arimathea...rolled a great stone to the door of the tomb and departed. Mary Magdalene and the other Mary were sitting there opposite the sepulcher." Matthew 27:6

*Hail Mary*

2. "The Pharisees gathered before Pilate and said: 'Sir, we remember how that Imposter said while He was still alive: "After three days I will rise again."'" Matthew 27:62-63

*Hail Mary*

3. "Pilate said to them: 'You have a guard of soldiers; go, make it as secure as you can.' So they went and made the sepulcher secure by sealing the stone and setting the guard." Matthew 27:65-66

*Hail Mary*

4. "And when the Sabbath was over, Mary Magdalene,

and Mary the mother of James, and Salome, brought spices.... Very early on the first day of the week they went to the tomb when the sun had risen." Mark 16:1-2

*Hail Mary*

5. "And looking up they saw that the stone was rolled back, for it was very large. And entering the tomb, they saw a young man...and they were amazed...." Mark 16:4

*Hail Mary*

6. "Do not be afraid! You seek Jesus of Nazareth, who was crucified. He has risen; He is not here.... But go tell His disciples and Peter...." Mark 16:6-7

*Hail Mary*

7. "Why do you seek the living among the dead? Remember how He told you: '...the Son of Man must be... crucified and on the third day rise.' And they remembered His words." Luke 24:5-8

*Hail Mary*

8. "(The women) told this to the Apostles, but...they didn't believe them." Luke 24:10-11

*Hail Mary*

9. "But Mary stood outside the tomb weeping.... She turned around and saw Jesus, but did not know that it was Jesus." John 20:11,14

*Hail Mary*

10. "Mary...go to My brethren and say to them: 'I am ascending to My Father and your Father, to My God and your God.' " John 20:17

*Hail Mary*

*Glory Be*

**The Ascension**

*Our Father*

1. "...He charged them not to depart from Jerusalem, but to wait for the Promise of the Father: '...before many days you shall be baptized with the Holy Spirit.'" Acts 1:4-5

*Hail Mary*

2. "When they had come together, they asked Him: 'Will You at this time restore the kingdom to Israel?'" Acts 1:6

*Hail Mary*

3. "It is not for you to know times or seasons which the Father has set by His own authority." Acts 1:7

*Hail Mary*

4. "...you shall receive power when the Holy Spirit has come upon you; and you shall be My witnesses...to the end of the earth." Acts 1:8

*Hail Mary*

5. "Then He led them out as far as Bethany, and lifting up His hands He blessed them." Luke 24:50

*Hail Mary*

6. "...as they were looking on, He was lifted up, and a cloud took Him out of their sight." Acts 1:9

*Hail Mary*

7. "And while they were gazing into heaven as He went, behold, two men in white robes stood by them." Acts 1:10

*Hail Mary*

8. "Men of Galilee, why do you stand looking into heaven? This Jesus who was taken up from you into heaven will

come in the same way as you saw Him go into heaven." Acts 1:11

*Hail Mary*

9. "Then they returned to Jerusalem from the mount called Olivet...and they went up to the upper room... where they devoted themselves to prayer, together with ...Mary the mother of Jesus...." Acts 1:12, 14

*Hail Mary*

10. "...Peter stood up among the brethren; (the company of persons was in all about a hundred and twenty)." Acts 1:15

*Hail Mary*

*Glory Be*

**The Descent of the Holy Spirit**

*Our Father*

1. "When the day of Pentecost had come, the were all together in one place. And suddenly a sound came from heaven like the rush of a mighty wind...." Acts 2:1-2

*Hail Mary*

2. "And there appeared to them tongues as of fire, parting and resting on each one of them." Acts 2:3-4

*Hail Mary*

3. "Now there were dwelling in Jerusalem devout Jews from every nation under heaven.... They were bewildered because each one heard them speaking in his own language." Acts 2:5-6

*Hail Mary*

4. "Peter standing with the eleven, lifted up his voice and addressed them: '...this is what was spoken by the prophet Joel: "God declares that in the last days, I will pour out My Spirit and they shall prophesy...and whoever calls on the Name of the Lord shall be saved."'" Acts 2:14, 16-17, 21

*Hail Mary*

5. "Men of Israel, hear these words: ...this Jesus, delivered up according to the definite plan and foreknowledge of God, you crucified and killed by the hands of lawless men. But God raised Him up." Acts 2:22-24

*Hail Mary*

6. "Being exalted at the right hand of God, and having received from the Father the promise of the Holy Spirit, He has poured out this which you now see and hear." Acts 2:33

*Hail Mary*

7. "...God has made Him both Lord and Christ, this Jesus whom you crucified. Now when they heard this, they were cut to the heart, and said to Peter and the rest of the Apostles: 'Brethren, what shall we do?'" Acts 2;36-37

*Hail Mary*

8. "Repent and be baptized, every one of you, in the name of the Lord Jesus Christ, for the forgiveness of your sins, and you shall receive the gift of the Holy Spirit." Acts 2:38

*Hail Mary*

9. "So those who received his word were baptized and there were added that day about three thousand souls...." Acts 2:41

*Hail Mary*

10. "And they devoted themselves to the Apostles' teaching and fellowship, to the breaking of the bread, and prayers." Acts 2:42

*Hail Mary*

*Glory Be*

**The Assumption of the Blessed Virgin Mary**

*Our Father*

1. "Mary said: 'My soul magnifies the Lord and my spirit rejoices in God my Savior....'" Luke 1:46-47

*Hail Mary*

2. "For He has regarded the lowliness of His handmaiden...." Luke 1:48

*Hail Mary*

3. "For behold, henceforth all generations shall call me blessed...." Luke 1:48

*Hail Mary*

4. "For He who is mighty has done great things for me, and holy is His name...." Luke 1:49

*Hail Mary*

5. "...and His mercy is on those who fear Him from generation to generation." Luke 1:50

*Hail Mary*

6. "He has shown strength with His arm. He has scattered the proud in the conceit of their hearts." Luke 1:51

*Hail Mary*

7. "He has put down the mighty from their thrones and exalted those of low degree...." Luke 1:52

*Hail Mary*

8. "He has filled the hungry with good things, and the rich He has sent empty away." Luke 1:53

*Hail Mary*

9. "He has helped His servant Israel, in remembrance of His mercy...." Luke 1:54

*Hail Mary*

10. "As He spoke to our fathers, to Abraham and to His posterity forever." Luke 1:55

*Hail Mary*

*Glory Be*

**The Coronation of Mary**

*Our Father*

1. "And the Lord God said to the Serpent: '...I will put enmities between you and the Woman, and your offspring and her Offspring...." Genesis 3:15

*Hail Mary*

2. "...He will crush your head, and you will lie in wait for His heel." Genesis 3:15

*Hail Mary*

3. "And a great sign appeared in heaven: a woman clothed with the sun, with the moon under her feet, and on her head a crown of twelve stars...." Revelation 12:1-2

*Hail Mary*

4. "...she was with Child and she cried out in her travail

of birth, in anguish for delivery." Revelation 12:3

*Hail Mary*

5. "And another sign appeared in heaven: a great red dragon...." Revelation 12:4

*Hail Mary*

6. "And the dragon stood before the woman, who was about to bear a Child, that he might devour her Child when she brought Him forth...." Revelation 12:4

*Hail Mary*

7. "She brought forth a male Child, one who is to rule all the nations with a rod of iron." Revelation 12:5

*Hail Mary*

8. "But her Child was caught up to God and to His throne." Revelation 12:15

*Hail Mary*

9. "And the woman fled into the wilderness, where she has a place prepared by God...." Revelation 12:6

*Hail Mary*

10. "The Spirit and the Bride say, 'Come.' And let him who hears say, 'Come.' ...Amen. Come, Lord Jesus!" Revelation 22:17, 20

*Hail Mary*

*Glory Be*

**Prayers after the Glorious Mysteries (and When All Twenty Decades of the Rosary Are Said at Once)**

1. Pray the Hail Holy Queen.
2. "Let us pray: O God - Whose Only Begotten Son by His Life, Death and Resurrection has purchased for us the rewards of eternal life – grant, we beseech You, that meditating on these Mysteries of the most holy Rosary of the Blessed Virgin Mary, we may imitate what they contain and obtain what they promise, through the same Christ our Lord. Amen."
3. Pray one Our Father, one Hail Mary and one Glory Be for the intention of the Holy Father.
4. Options:
   a. "May the Divine Assistance remain always with us. And may the souls of the faithful departed, through the mercy of God, rest in peace. Amen."
   b. "May the Sacred Heart of Jesus, in the Most Blessed Sacrament of the Altar, be praised adored and loved, with grateful affection, at every moment, in all the tabernacles of the world, even to the end of time. Amen."
   c. "St. Michael the Archangel, defend us in battle. Be our safeguard against the wickedness and snares of the devil. Rebuke him, O God, we humbly pray and do you, O Prince of the Heavenly Hosts, by the power of God, cast into hell Satan and all the evil spirits who roam about the world seeking the ruin of souls. Amen."
5. On the crucifix, make the Sign of the Cross, while praying: "In the Name of the Father, and of the Son, and of the Holy Spirit. Amen."

## *Traditional Prayers Used in This Book*

**Lord's Prayer**

Our Father, who art in heaven, hallowed be Thy Name. Thy kingdom come, Thy will be done, on earth as it is in heaven. Give us this day our daily bread and forgive us our trespasses as we forgive those who trespass against us. And lead us not into temptation, but deliver us from evil. Amen.

**Hail Mary**

Hail Mary, full of grace, the Lord is with thee. Blessed are thou among women and blessed is the fruit of thy womb, Jesus. Holy Mary, Mother of God, pray for us sinners now and at the hour of our death. Amen.

**Glory Be**

Glory be to the Father, and to the Son, and to the Holy Spirit: As it was in the beginning, is now, and ever shall be, world without end. Amen.

**Apostles' Creed**

I believe in God, the Father Almighty, creator of heaven and earth. And in Jesus Christ, his only Son, our Lord, who was conceived of the Holy Spirit and born of the Virgin Mary, suffered under Pontius Pilate, was crucified, died, and was buried. He descended into hell; on the third day he rose again from the dead. He ascended into heaven, and is seated at the right hand of the Father, from whence He shall come again to judge the living and the dead. I believe in the Holy Spirit, the holy catholic Church, the communion of saints, the forgiveness of sins, the resurrection of the body, and life everlasting. Amen.

**Hail Holy Queen**

Hail Holy Queen, Mother of Mercy, our life, our sweetness, and our hope. To you do we cry, poor banished children of Eve. To you do we send up our sighs, mourning and weeping in this valley of tears. Turn then, most gracious advocate, your eyes of mercy toward us, and after this, our exile, show unto us the blessed fruit of your womb, Jesus. O clement, O loving, O sweet Virgin Mary.

Pray for us, O Holy Mother of God, that we may be made worthy of the promises of Christ. Amen.